WELCOME TO WONDERSTRUCK 1977

On the following pages, you will learn how my book *Wonderstruck* was turned into a movie. Half the story takes place in 1977, and you'll see how a team of artists (including me!) worked together to re-create that year, when a boy named Ben becomes deaf and runs away from home.

BUT WAIT! THERE'S MORE!

You are actually holding *two* books in one, because *Wonderstruck* is like two *movies* in one. If you turn this book over, you will discover *Wonderstruck: 1927*, where you will learn how those same artists worked together to re-create the other half of the movie, which takes place in 1927, when a Deaf girl named Rose runs away from home.

The movie follows both of these stories, in 1977 and 1927, until they ultimately come together. This book will do the same.

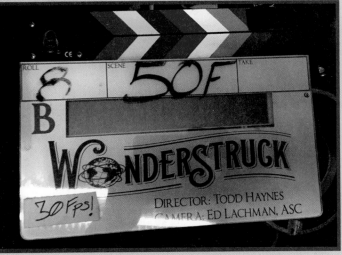

This is the "clapper," used to mark the start and finish of every scene filmed in the movie.

Being a part of the extraordinary movie-making process left me wonderstruck, and I hope this book will show you why!
— Brian Selznick

The crew films on a street in Brooklyn, New York, that has been designed to look like Times Square in 1977.

Oakes Fegley filming on location at the American Museum of Natural History.

Jaden Michael, as Jamie, with his character's Polaroid camera.

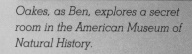

Oakes, as Ben, explores a secret room in the American Museum of Natural History.

Jaden films a scene in front of a fake wall. In the movie it will look like he's walking on a street in New York City.

TABLE OF CONTENTS

This is my book *Wonderstruck*, which I wrote and illustrated. For the movie, I wrote the screenplay (my first!), and had a fantastic and challenging time adapting the story from the page to the screen. In a book, there are usually three ways to tell a story: with words, with pictures, or with a combination of both. But in a movie there are many tools to work with: dialogue, pictures (in 3-D sometimes), black and white, color, music, lighting, editing, sound, and silence. Imagine a busy street with many loud noises and honking cars and screaming people, then imagine the same scene with all the sound removed. In a movie you can do that, and lots of other moviemaking tricks, too!

Me with actors Oakes Fegley and Jaden Michael.

A page from my screenplay.

INT. MINNESOTA HOSPITAL – ROOM – NEXT MORNING   *

SILENCE.

Ben's face. His eyes wide open.

Hands appear and pull a white sheet up to his neck.

Ben looks to his left. A nurse is standing next to him. A
machine is blinking.

AUNT JENNY is standing near the bed, dressed in her work
uniform (her name, *"Jenny,"* stitched into her brown blouse).
She looks exhausted and scared, as Janet looks on beside her.
Robby sits sulking in the corner. Aunt Jenny strokes Ben's
hair and speaks to him, but we don't hear any sound.

Ben looks back, and tries to reply, but the sound of his
voice has been replaced by a deeply buried echo.

> BEN
> Where am I? What happened?

It sounds more like the memory of a voice than anything
anyone could actually hear.

> BEN (CONT'D)
> What's wrong? (He taps
> ear) Hello? Hello?

Aunt Jenny puts a finger to her ~~n~~
indicating that *she* can hear *him.*

The nurse hands Jenny a clipboar~~d~~
a pen. Aunt Jenny writes somethi~~ng~~
written to Ben:

You're OK. You had an accident.

Ben doesn't understand.

Jenny crosses out what she wrote,
Ben can see and <u>draws</u> a simple h~~ouse~~
on top. She adds a curly telepho~~ne~~
holding the line to his ear.

*When Ben loses his hearing,
we used silence, creative
sound design, and unusual
music to represent what
he experiences.*

W hen I was first writing the book *Wonder-struck*, I originally chose to set part of the story in 1977 because it was the year of a famous blackout in New York City. In fact, the blackout started on July 13 and continued through my eleventh birthday, on the fourteenth. I remember seeing the headlines in the newspapers.

This is me in 1976. In the summer of 1977, I turned eleven, the same age as the main character, Ben.

This is a drawing of the blackout from my book.

RATIONS

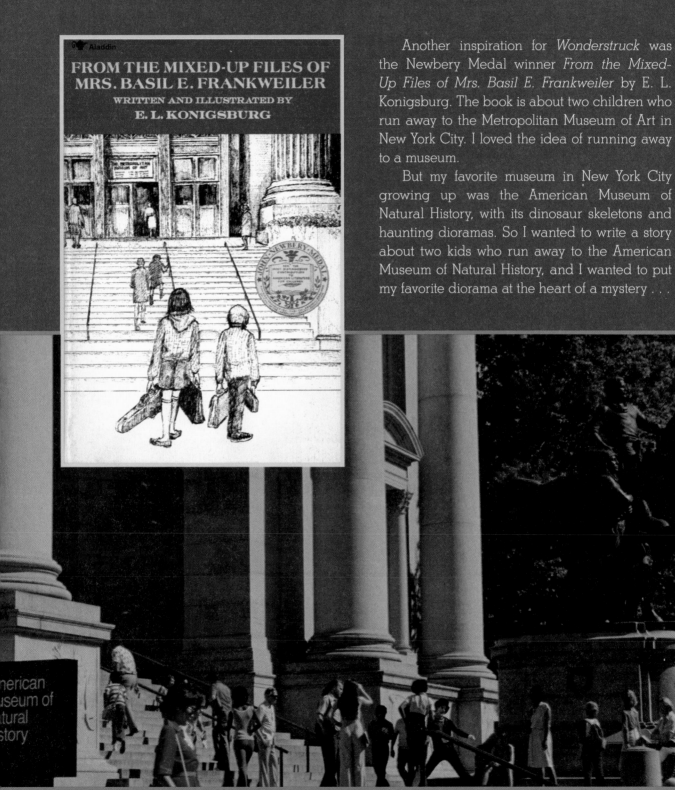

FROM THE MIXED-UP FILES OF MRS. BASIL E. FRANKWEILER

WRITTEN AND ILLUSTRATED BY
E. L. KONIGSBURG

Another inspiration for *Wonderstruck* was the Newbery Medal winner *From the Mixed-Up Files of Mrs. Basil E. Frankweiler* by E. L. Konigsburg. The book is about two children who run away to the Metropolitan Museum of Art in New York City. I loved the idea of running away to a museum.

But my favorite museum in New York City growing up was the American Museum of Natural History, with its dinosaur skeletons and haunting dioramas. So I wanted to write a story about two kids who run away to the American Museum of Natural History, and I wanted to put my favorite diorama at the heart of a mystery . . .

The entrance to the American Museum of Natural History, with set decorations, including 1970s signage and people in costume, to make it look like it did in 1977.

For as long as I can remember, I've been especially intrigued by this wolf diorama, with its two wolves running at night by the light of the moon. The diorama is set in Gunflint Lake, Minnesota. When I started doing research for the book, I thought, *I wonder if the people of Gunflint Lake know this diorama is here. What if a boy from Gunflint Lake found himself in New York City and one day wandered into the American Museum of Natural History and discovered this connection to his home?*

A close-up view of the wolf diorama at the American Museum of Natural History.

NOBODY DOES
Todd Haynes Dire

Todd Haynes directs Oakes Fegley as Ben.

Julianne Moore with her friend Todd Haynes on the set.

Todd Haynes is a famous director who has created many award-winning movies. As the director, Todd is in charge of telling the story on-screen. He collaborates with many people, from the screenwriter to the production designer, costume designer, actors, cinematographer, and others. It's the director's vision and ideas that everyone is trying to help bring to life. *Wonderstruck* is Todd's first movie for a family audience, and he was really excited about making it.

One of Todd's favorite actresses to work with is Oscar-winner Julianne Moore. They've made four movies together, and she plays two different characters in *Wonderstruck*. "I like everything about working with Todd," said Julianne. "Todd has a love and enthusiasm for moviemaking that is palpable!"

IT BETTER
cts *Wonderstruck*

Todd in high school in 1976. He was already making movies.

> **"When we fill a movie in with our emotions as spectators it becomes powerful and alive."**
> **— Todd Haynes**

"I've made films that have been set in the seventies before," Todd said. "I think there was a lot of amazing stuff going on culturally." One of the first movies Todd directed, *Superstar*, was also set in the 1970s. It is about a famous singer, but instead of using actors, he used Barbie dolls! Even though the movie is made with toys, it's not for children. It deals with serious, grown-up themes. In *Superstar*, the dolls feel like real people, with real emotions. As a kid, I loved miniatures and dolls and I really believed my dolls were alive. To create *Wonderstruck*, Todd brilliantly used his own connection with toys, childhood, and memory.

Todd directs Oakes amid a crowd of extras dressed in 1970s costumes.

Before filming *Wonderstruck*, Todd watched many other movies for inspiration and research. From 1970s movies like *The French Connection* to older movies with great performances by children such as *How Green Was My Valley*, *The Night of the Hunter*, and *To Kill a Mockingbird*, Todd recommended that the entire cast and crew watch many of the same movies so everyone would understand what he was trying to do with *Wonderstruck*. These old movies became a shared language for everyone on the set.

Mary Badham and Gregory Peck in To Kill a Mockingbird *(1962), directed by Robert Mulligan. Mary was nine years old when she filmed this movie.*

Roddy McDowall and Walter Pidgeon in How Green Was My Valley *(1941), directed by John Ford. Roddy was twelve years old when he filmed this movie.*

Sally Jane Bruce and Billy Chapin with Robert Mitchum in The Night of the Hunter *(1955), directed by Charles Laughton. Billy was ten years old and Sally was five years old when they filmed this movie.*

PIRATIONS

> "Todd is a super-awesome director who likes to understand how you feel with the character, and he lets you put in your own flavor to it. I will carry forever all his great teachings that he shared with me. He also has an amazing charisma and is always happy and smiling!" — Jaden Michael

Actor Jaden Michael was twelve years old when he filmed Wonderstruck.

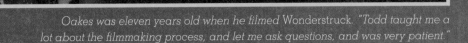

Oakes was eleven years old when he filmed Wonderstruck. *"Todd taught me a lot about the filmmaking process, and let me ask questions, and was very patient."*

Friends Forever

Oakes Fegley and Jaden Michael Discover
What It's Like to Be Friends in 1977 New York

Oakes Fegley and Jaden Michael, the actors who play Ben and Jamie in the movie, became friends in real life, just as their characters do in the movie. Like Ben and Jamie, Oakes and Jaden come from different places: Oakes lives in Allentown, Pennsylvania, and Jaden in New York City. The two boys hit it off right away. "Jaden is super fun," said Oakes. "He's a really good actor, and it was very cool getting to work with him. He's a very caring person." Jaden said, "We had fun playing video games and card games when we weren't filming."

Jaden and Oakes with Todd on the set.

> "Ben's searching for where he belongs, and I can relate to that." — Oakes Fegley

Oakes loved filming in Ben's house. Can you see how the ceiling was removed in order to allow the movie camera to film from above?

Jaden particularly enjoyed the secret storage room in the American Museum of Natural History. "I loved all the attention that was put into that room," said Jaden, "like the cool Polaroids on the wall and the buttons my character collected. It kind of mirrored what I was imagining!"

Jaden and Oakes during filming. Can you spot the sound man with the boom microphone?

Jaden, Millie, and Oakes.

Oakes and Jaden also had fun hanging out with Millicent Simmonds, who plays young Rose in 1927. See page 34 in *Wonderstruck: 1927* to read more about their friendship, and how Oakes and Jaden started learning sign language to communicate with Millie, who is Deaf.

Oakes and Jaden filming near the wolf diorama in the American Museum of Natural History.

Jaden relaxing during a break. In the background you can see some of the trailers where the actors got into their costumes or had their hair and makeup done.

Oakes and Jaden had to run up and down a lot of steps while making the movie!

PLEASE, SIR, MAY I

Twice the Fun! Actress Julianne Moore

Before she was cast in *Wonderstruck*, the Oscar-winning actress Julianne Moore was already a fan of the book, and had hoped to play older Rose. Little did she know that one day her friend Todd Haynes would direct the movie, and ask her to play not only older Rose (who is Deaf), but another character as well.

Julianne Moore wore specially designed age makeup to play older Rose!

HAVE SOME MOORE!
Plays TWO Characters in *Wonderstruck*

Tom Noonan (who plays the older Walter), Julianne, and Todd in Kincaid's Books, which was filmed in a bookstore on the Upper West Side of Manhattan that inspired me when I was writing my book. It used to be called Gryphon Books, but now it's called Westsider Books. Visit if you can!

Julianne and Oakes filming on the Panorama at the Queens Museum (see page 36 to learn more about the Panorama). In this scene, both characters are Deaf but only one of them knows sign language. Therefore they communicate using written notes.

"In my work, I get to learn so much about other people," Julianne said. "That, to me, has been the most surprising and, ultimately, most satisfying part of being an actor. When we are playing characters different from ourselves (as we almost always are), it is our responsibility to learn as much as we can so that we are able to be as truthful as possible about our characters."

To prepare for her role as Rose, Julianne worked closely with Deaf teacher and actress Alexandria Wailes for several months. "Alexandria was so incredibly kind and generous with me. She was funny and patient and challenged me to be as precise as possible in my work. She taught me American Sign Language (ASL) but also so much about Deaf history and culture. Before we even began learning basic signing, she asked me if I knew the origins of ASL, which she signed to me while I tried to follow! I loved it it was like being thrown into the deep end right away.

"Learning about Deaf culture and American Sign Language was so stimulating and incredibly informative," said Julianne. "I came away with an understanding and appreciation for ASL as a language, and my new Deaf friends gave me insight into a culture that I had not been introduced to and wouldn't have been otherwise introduced to."

Award-winning actress Michelle Williams has played all sorts of fascinating, complex characters, including the actress Marilyn Monroe! In *Wonderstruck*, she plays Ben's mother, Elaine Wilson. In real life, Michelle has a young daughter. Filming the movie made her think a lot about what it means to be a parent.

Thinking about Ben, she said, "He sets out on his life's journey earlier than most and finds the inner reserves and abiding friendships that will see him through. Maybe this is why children find the story so absorbing. Because it says that no matter what happens in life, they will find their way."

Michelle Williams appears in flashbacks as Ben's mom. The character of Elaine was named after the author of From the Mixed-Up Files of Mrs. Basil E. Frankweiler, *E. L. Konigsburg. The "E." stands for "Elaine."*

BELLE

Michelle Williams Plays a Haunting Character

Elaine comes to Ben's room on his birthday with a gift.

Elaine Wilson collects all sorts of quotes and photographs, which she hangs in her room. The quote on the blue card, from a writer named Oscar Wilde, is very important to her, and to the story.

We are all in the gutter, but some of us are looking at the stars.

Mark Friedberg Re-creat

Mark Friedberg is the production designer for the movie. He was responsible for designing all the *places* in the movie, every street, storefront, house, apartment, and museum. Sometimes he built a place from scratch, other times he found a real location and used that.

A big part of Mark's job was making New York City look like it did when he was a kid back in 1977. He especially remembered how dirty it used to be. So when it was time to decorate the sets, Mark had to keep telling his crew: "More garbage! More trash! More rubble!"

There were a lot of burned-out, abandoned cars in New York City back then.

Mark instructs his crew to make the sets dirtier.

Mark captured the grittiness and dirt he remembers so well.

More garbage! All the garbage was handmade so it would be accurate to the year 1977.

RA! GARBAGE!
es the World of His Youth

We were allowed to film some scenes for the movie on location at the American Museum of Natural History. The tracks you see are for the camera, so it can glide smoothly through the room.

We were honored to film on location at the American Museum of Natural History in New York City. We spent several nights there after hours, alone with just a few security guards and the crew. It was magical! But there were some scenes we couldn't film at the museum, so a few rooms were re-created in a movie studio. For instance, the real workshop in the museum, where the exhibitions are built, was off-limits because they were using it. So we had to build a fake one. When you watch the movie, you'll never know that the actors might be walking through a door in the museum and entering a room in a completely different building across the city.

Besides the museum, we filmed all over New York. Very often, Mark found a location that looked interesting and then he'd transform it using signs or posters until it looked like someplace else.

Jaden Michael on the set that was created to look like a workshop at the American Museum of Natural History.

Oakes Fegley as Ben in Times Square. This scene was actually filmed in Brooklyn.

Mark Friedberg as a boy in New York City in the 1970s.

Mark, like me, was inspired as a young boy by the American Museum of Natural History and its dioramas. He said, "Dioramas are like incredibly short films. They have everything to do with what happened *before* the moment you're seeing, and what's about to happen next. I grew up in this museum, staring at the dioramas. It's what I wanted to do as a kid. I wanted to make dioramas."

Most of *Wonderstruck* takes place in New York City, but the movie opens in a small town in Minnesota called Gunflint Lake. When I was making the book I went to Gunflint Lake to do research. But Mark and the movie crew were unable to travel there, so they found places in New York State that looked similar. Even though the story opens in Minnesota, it was really filmed at a cabin in Carmel, New York!

Ben's house in Gunflint Lake, Minnesota, was actually filmed in Carmel, New York.

26

Oakes Fegley filming at the wolf diorama
in the American Museum of Natural History.

The workshop where the sets were built from scratch.

The movie studio during filming.

NOW YOU SEE IT
The Visual Effects of Louis Morin

ouis Morin is the visual effects supervisor for the movie. "My specialty," said Louis, "has always been to make invisible visual effects that blend seamlessly into the film where you have no idea what is real and what is digital."

For example, when we filmed this scene, we weren't really in Times Square. We were in Brooklyn. Signs and storefronts were designed to help make it look like Times Square. But do you see all the green trees in the first picture? In the real Times Square there were no trees, so Louis and his team digitally replaced the trees with buildings to make it appear as though the scene takes place in Times Square in 1977. Look closely at the finished shot from the movie. Would you have ever guessed that some of these buildings are not real?

This is what the scene in Times Square looked like before any visual effects were added.

This is the finished shot from the movie.

SANDY POWELL FEVER

The Costume Designer Who Sets New York Ablaze

Costume designer Sandy Powell has won three Oscars and designed costumes for more than forty-five movies, including Disney's *Cinderella*. Sandy often begins designing costumes by looking at real vintage clothing. She also looks at lots of images from the time period in which the movie takes place. For Jaden Michael's costume, she found a vintage shirt and had it re-created several times, so if one got dirty while filming, they had another one ready to go.

Sandy Powell amid the crowds of Times Square.

The pants were harder because she couldn't find any children's pants from the time period to fit Jaden, and she couldn't just buy a new pair because the type of denim fabric used in jeans has changed since the seventies. Luckily, she came across a giant pair of grown-up pants with the right type of denim. She and her team cut up the giant pants and made a pair for Jaden that was the right style and fit for 1977!

Sandy Makes a Costume

Sandy begins to think about actor Jaden Michael's costume.

Sandy finds the right denim in the wrong size.

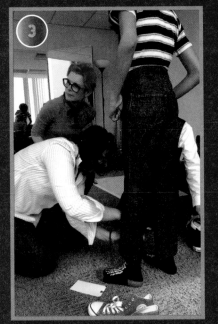

Jaden at a costume fitting.

Jaden tries to get his pants on! Clothing in the seventies was very tight.

The finished costume on Jaden in the movie.

"Costumes are incredibly important to an actor. Clothes are one of the many ways that people communicate who they are. So you really have to feel that your costumes are contributing to telling a story about your character. Luckily, we have one of the best costume designers in the whole movie business!" — Julianne Moore

Jaden Michael and Julianne Moore in costume, talking with director Todd Haynes.

Sandy Powell in the seventies.

In the costume department, real jewelry from the seventies was collected for all the extras.

Sandy knew there was a heat wave during the summer of 1977, so most of the costumes for the New Yorkers in Times Square were very skimpy or thin. But the day we filmed this scene, it was really cold outside! The extras all needed blankets during the breaks.

Extras trying to stay warm while filming the heat wave on the Times Square set.

Every single detail is important to Sandy.

Sandy amid rows and rows of costumes.

This is Ed Lachman, the cinematographer for *Wonderstruck*. His job is to light the sets, the costumes, and the actors. He's in charge of the cameras, and he helps the director decide on the best lenses to capture the look of the movie.

Did you ever notice when you watch an old movie that it *looks* like an old movie? Movies from different time periods have different styles and were made on different types of film stock, and that affected what they looked like. Ed helped Todd make the story in 1977 look like it was actually *filmed* in 1977. Ed said, "We wanted to reference the time period through cinema!"

Ed had a lot of challenges lighting this movie, especially when it came to filming the Panorama at the Queens Museum. The Panorama is a 10,000-square-foot model of the entire city of New York, and it plays a big part in the story.

Ed Lachman with his camera.

Using special film stock and lighting, Ed really captured the feeling of the movies in 1977.

THE LIGHT!
oots and Scores

The movie *The French Connection*, made in 1971, was a big influence on *Wonderstruck*. Ed tried to capture the look of this movie. He even called the original cinematographer of *The French Connection*, Owen Roizman, to ask him how he filmed it, including what lenses he used. There is also a car chase in *Wonderstruck*, though our car chase is very short. Look for it at the very end of the movie!

A professional drone pilot was hired to fly cameras in order to film the Panorama from above.

Film still from The French Connection, *which was a big inspiration to Ed.*

Director Todd Haynes rests on a specially constructed platform so he can show Ed how he wants to film the Panorama without damaging it.

SMALL TOWN, NEW YORK
The Panorama at the Queens Museum

Built for the 1964 New York World's Fair, the Panorama has 895,000 buildings on it, and it can still be seen at the Queens Museum. Louise Weinberg, the Registrar and Archives Manager, helped me research the Panorama for my book and then helped with the movie, too. Louise provided us with rare photos of the Panorama being built that were used by the art department, and she gave us access to the model itself, which no one is normally allowed to walk on.

Louise hopes the film will bring more awareness to the world of the Panorama and that even more people will come to visit it. She said, "The Panorama is incredible, and everyone should experience what a unique thing it is for themselves."

A tiny Empire State Building rises from the Panorama.

Older Rose carefully steps over a bridge on the Panorama in a scene from the movie.

The creation of the Panorama in 1963 from the Queens Museum's archives.

Every fifteen minutes, night falls across the Panorama. To make it seem as if the lights come on, every window on the Panorama is painted with special paint and illuminated by hidden fluorescent lights.

LITTLE
Memory and Miniatures Colli

At the end of *Wonderstruck*, there's a long series of flashbacks where one character tells a story about what she's been doing for the last fifty years. The filmmakers had a huge challenge figuring out how to show this on-screen. Finally, Mark Friedberg, the production designer, and Todd Haynes, the director, had the idea to shoot the entire sequence of events in miniature, like dioramas in a museum. I thought this was such a great idea because so much of the story takes place in a museum.

Katrina Whalen, who has a background in stop-motion animation and in-camera effects, and who had worked with Mark on several other movies, was brought in to develop and produce the miniature sequence with Todd and Mark. Robert Pyzocha's team of model makers created the exquisitely detailed sets, and animator Hayley Morris and her team created an army of miniature "actors." Altogether, they created nineteen miniature sets and over 300 characters, spanning more than 50 years in the life of Rose. "Our scale for most of the models was: every foot in the real world would be an inch in our scale. So all of the characters are about five to six inches high, and all of our ceilings are eight to twelve inches from the floor. Mark Friedberg continually pushed us to enrich the design of the sets—each of them was so beautifully conceived and constructed."

Miniature workers at the American Museum of Natural History. This was inspired by a scene in the 1928 movie The Crowd.

WONDERS
de at the End of *Wonderstruck*

A crew member puts final touches on a miniature school before filming.

Actress Millicent Simmonds and I inspect some of the miniature models in the workshop.

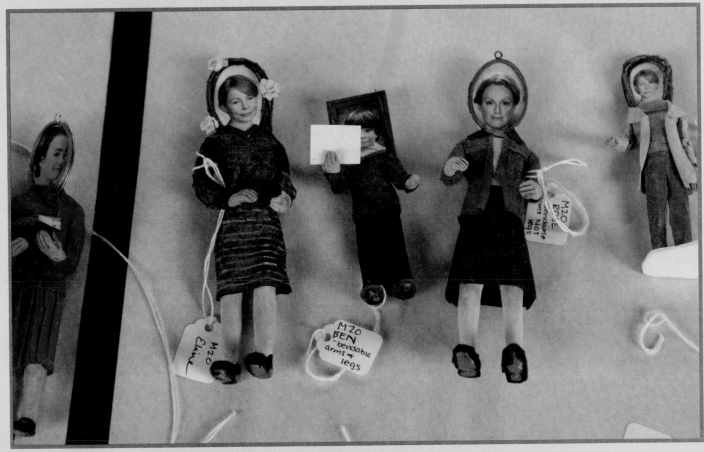

Puppets created for the miniature sequence at the end of the movie.

The crew films a moonlit miniature landscape, covered in fake snow. The moonlight was created with the sheets above the diorama, and the film camera can be seen on the end of a mechanical arm on the right side of the forest. The red toy truck is hidden by the trees!

Todd had so much fun filming the miniature sequence; it reminded him of making his movie, *Superstar*. With *Wonderstruck*, Todd's movies have come full circle. He wanted to fill the miniature sequence with elements that would connect the miniatures to the rest of the movie. "There are objects in Ben's bedroom," Todd told me, "like a red toy truck sitting on his nightstand that becomes the red truck that his father is driving up the snowy path to first meet his mother in one of the flashbacks." Many people may not notice these visual connections, but if you watch the movie more than once, you might find more objects that appear in Ben's room and the museum that reappear in the miniatures!

There's even a miniature of the wolf diorama with an even more miniature wolf diorama in it!

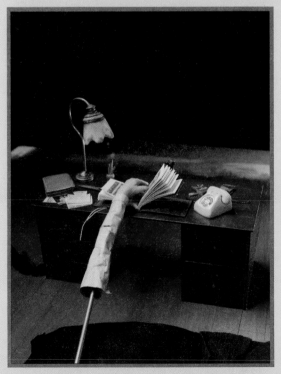

A puppet hand turns the pages of a tiny book.

Todd with a very small diorama.

The crew filming a miniature sequence set in a Deaf school in the 1920s. Do you see the person sitting under the table, ready to help make the miniature school come to life? That is a puppeteer.

BUT SOME OF US ARE LOOKING AT THE STARS!

Jaden Michael, on the night we finished filming.

The story of *Wonderstruck* is about finding your place in the world and creating your own family. On the last night of filming, when Todd yelled, "Cut!" and we knew we were finished, everyone cheered and burst into tears. There were lots of hugs, and as I looked around at everyone, I realized we'd all formed a kind of family. I made so many new friends on this movie, and felt so lucky to be a part of it all.

But the movie wasn't done yet. Affonso Gonçalves needed to edit the film, Carter Burwell needed to compose the music, Leslie Shatz needed to do the sound, and many others had lots of work to do as well. In all, it took about eight more months. Now the movie is done and ready to be seen by you. I hope you enjoy watching it as much as I enjoyed being a part of its making.

WELCOME TO
WONDERSTRUCK
1927

O n the following pages, you will learn how my book *Wonderstruck* was turned into a movie. Half the story takes place in 1927, and you'll see how a team of artists (including me!) worked together to re-create that year, when a Deaf girl named Rose runs away from home.

But Wait! There's More!

You are actually holding *two* books in one, because *Wonderstruck* is like two *movies* in one. If you turn this book over, you will discover *Wonderstruck: 1977*, where you will see how those same artists worked together to re-create the other half of the movie, which takes place in 1977, when a boy named Ben becomes deaf and runs away from home.

The movie follows both of these stories, in 1927 and 1977, until they ultimately come together. This book will do the same.

This is me on the set of the ferry terminal where Rose leaves for New York City. Do you see the old-fashioned car in the background? The movie rented about 500 cars during the filming, for authenticity.

I hope you'll find yourself wonderstruck!
— Brian Selznick

I have a cameo in the movie. Here I am (in costume) with actress Julianne Moore and director Todd Haynes.

TABLE OF CONTENTS

HOW IT ALL BEGAN ~
The Inspiration Behind the Book

This is the cover of my book *Wonderstruck*, which was the basis for the movie. When I started writing the book, I knew I wanted to write two stories about Deaf characters. But I didn't know which years the stories would take place, until I remembered that 1927 was the year that sound was introduced to moving pictures.

Before 1927, all moving pictures were "silent movies." When film was first invented, the technology to add sound didn't exist, so the stories were acted out visually. If characters were having a conversation, the words would sometimes be *written* on the screen on what are called "title cards."

Music was usually played live in the movie theater, on an organ or by an orchestra, but the music was never essential to the story and it was different in every theater. Before 1927, Deaf people could attend all popular movies of the day and understand them. But when sound was introduced, title cards disappeared, and Deaf people suddenly found themselves unable to follow the story.

In my book, I decided to tell the story of a Deaf person, Rose, with just drawings. I wanted it to reflect the way she experienced her own life: visually.

A Sequence of Drawings

1.

2. ARTCRAFT PICTURES PRESENTS
DAUGHTER of THE STORM

3.

4.

5. STAR RING
Lillian MAYHEW

6. "Oh no! The storm is here!"

This sequence from my book Wonderstruck *shows Rose watching a silent movie in 1927. Note the title card that shows the dialogue.*

A page from my screenplay.

Rose moves along amid the great sea of bodies, clutching her bag as she goes.

EXT. NEW YORK CITY - 1927 - DAY

Rose turns and finds herself in the flow of a bustling downtown street.

A river of sharp clothes and brisk walkers, leather purses and black lunch-boxes, lead her along. Smart stores flickering by, smart women with short bobs and tight cloches. And a stream of businessmen in flat straw-hats and fedoras.

Rose continues on, caught between the seamless flow and the constant jostle, the snaking traffic and corner venders (one woman with long hair selling flowers at the corner), dwarfed and elevated by everything she sees.

She suddenly looks up - and what a sight! Buildings jutting into the sky, grande facades and streamline splendor. Chrome and steel, brick and stone. Hard sharp shadows.

In the distance, the jutting spines of new construction, shooting lines of steel into the sky.

Dizzy with the sights Rose walks headlong into a horse and carriage making a sudden turn onto a cross-street, as people shout and drivers pound their horns.

                    VOICES
          Stop! Look out! What are you doing?

Startled, she falls backwards into a MALE PEDESTRIAN, and hits the ground. The Pedestrian glances back annoyedly as he marches on.

Rose watches as the crowd resumes its busy pace, marching past her, oblivious.

Rose arriving in New York in 1927. Rose is played by young Deaf actress Millicent Simmonds.

TODD HAYNES M
Famous Film Director Takes on Hi

The director's job is to bring everything in the screenplay to life. In fact, even though I made up the story, I would say that the movie truly belongs to the director. I've been a huge fan of Todd's since his first big movie came out in 1991 (the same year my first book was published!). I was thrilled that he wanted to direct *Wonderstruck*. Todd said, "It was a powerful experience for me, reading it." He's often made movies about characters who are alone or outsiders, and that perfectly describes Ben, Jamie, and Rose in *Wonderstruck*.

Todd worked closely with me to finish the screenplay. Then he collaborated with the production designer, the costume designer, the actors, the cinematographer, and all the others who helped create the movie. He made sure that everyone understood his vision and was working to tell the same story in the best way possible.

Todd directing actress Millicent Simmonds on location at the American Museum of Natural History.

AKES A MOVIE
s First-Ever Movie for Children

Todd (center) on the soundstage, where many of our sets were built.

Todd with cinematographer Ed Lachman.

Todd (center) with the camera crew while filming a scene on a street that was made to look like Manhattan in 1927.

Todd with actress Millicent Simmonds and her sign language interpreter, Lynnette Taylor.

BLACK AND WHITE AND READ ALL OVER
Learning from the Movies

Director Todd Haynes was excited about the idea of filming *Wonderstruck* in two different styles. He watched many silent movies from the 1920s for inspiration, such as *Sunrise* by F. W. Murnau (1927), King Vidor's *The Crowd* (1928), and *The Wind* by Victor Sjöström (1928). "These were films that had very specific relevance to our story and setting," said Todd. "They were inspirational for the way the film would look and feel in 1927 New York, a poetic, subjective reality of Rose's experience that would contrast the grittier, harder-edged experience of Ben in the seventies."

Rose travels through New York City in 1927 in a scene inspired by F. W. Murnau's movie Sunrise.

A scene from Sunrise, *made in 1927 by F. W. Murnau.*

A scene from King Vidor's The Crowd, *made in 1928.*

Todd with miniature desks built for a scene in Wonderstruck, *inspired by* The Crowd.

Silent movie star Lillian Gish in The Wind, *from 1928.*

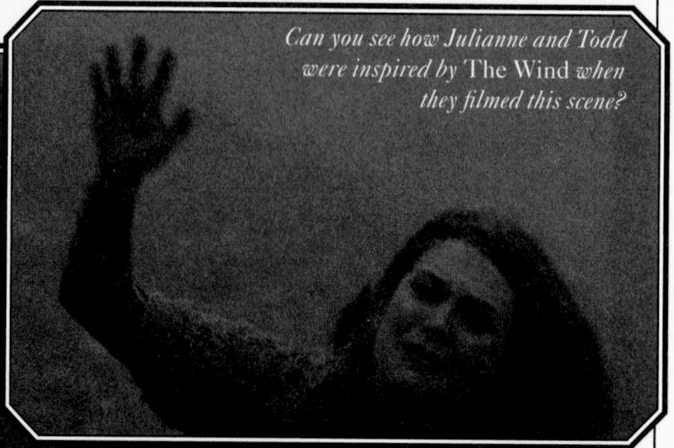

Can you see how Julianne and Todd were inspired by The Wind *when they filmed this scene?*

"Some scholars say that cinema reached its highest level of sophistication right before the onset of sound." — Todd Haynes

EVERYTHING'S C
Brilliant Young Newcomer Takes

Millicent Simmonds plays young Rose in *Wonderstruck*. "We received about two hundred audition tapes from young Deaf girls," said Todd Haynes. "But there was something about Millie. We all stood up and took notice."

Millie was already a fan of the book when she was cast as Rose, and she was especially excited because she has a larger message she wants to share with people. "I want this movie to show the world that Deaf* kids can do everything," she told me in American Sign Language. "I want to show hearing and Deaf people that we can all come together. I am PROUD to be Deaf."

Rose walking through New York City. Millie hadn't been to New York City before being cast in this movie. "Rose's amazement when she saw the city was the same as mine when I came here," she recalled.

---

*Regarding the capitalization of the word "Deaf": "We use the lowercase deaf when referring to the audiological condition of not hearing, and the uppercase Deaf when referring to a particular group of deaf people who share a language—American Sign Language (ASL)—and a culture."
— From *Deaf in America: Voices from a Culture* by Carol Padden and Tom Humphries

OMING UP ROSES
Starring Role in Moving Picture

Sometimes on the set Todd would show Millie what her character needed to do. Millie did it perfectly every time!

2 things about me:
1. I love my family a lot! ☺

2. I love to be Deaf. Sign Language is Awesome and Beautiful!!

In her original audition tape, Millie used sign language, then she showed cue cards to translate what she'd said.

Millie found it easy to work with director Todd Haynes. "He is really nice. He knows how to work with Deaf people. He knows how to sign the words 'action,' 'rolling,' 'cut.'"

Millie related to the character of Rose. "She had such a hard time. Sad and hard," she signed to me, "but also happy because she escaped and learned she can do anything, so I wanted to help Todd make Rose come to life. I wanted to become Rose, to really feel what Rose felt. I understood how Rose was frustrated with a father that forced her to speak. Todd would tell me to really think about Rose and how she would feel and what was in her mind. There have been a lot of times when I would visit my extended family or cousins and they would never look me in the eye or even notice me. No one would try and communicate with me. I would really get frustrated and even angry and think, *Why? Being deaf wasn't my choice. Why are they acting like I'm not even here?* But my immediate family accepts me and learned sign language for me. Rose didn't have that. She must have felt so alone. For years. Way more than me. I would try and reach that feeling and hold on to that feeling while I was on set."

Millie had fun learning about all the equipment it takes to make a movie. Here she tries to control a camera rig. It's heavy!

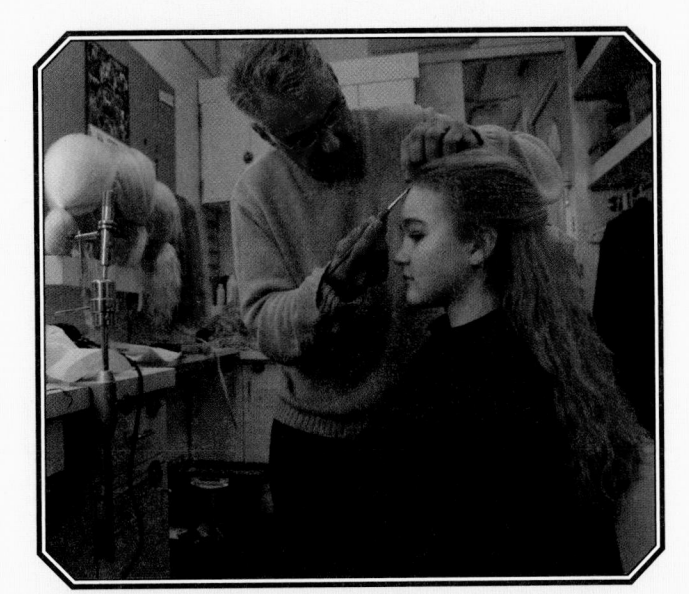

In real life Millie had short hair, so for the beginning of the movie she wore a specially made wig.

Mustaches were popular with Millie, who loved to play practical jokes on the set.

"She's a profoundly talented, deeply sensitive, intelligent, vital person. We just lucked out in every conceivable way with Millie!" — Todd Haynes

Millie made sure that the character of Rose was brave and independent.

Millie was excited to work with actress Julianne Moore. "Julianne learned a lot of awesome sign language. I am really proud of her. She is so sweet, funny, fun. She is amazing. When I was a little kid I always looked up to her. I always wanted to be like her. And now, here I am working with her! How crazy is that?"

Julianne Moore practices her sign language with Millie on the set.

"Millie was a thrill to work with. She has such a strong personality, and is a natural actor. It was hard for me to believe that she had never acted before because she was so comfortable in front of a camera, and truly lights up the screen! Also, she gave me my ASL name! Millie was so kind and encouraging to me about my signing." — Julianne Moore

Me and Millie's mom, Emily, watch as Millie films her very last scene in Wonderstruck.

Millie, Todd, and Lynnette on the set. Lynnette remembers how happy the young actress was. "Millie kept saying over and over, 'I feel so welcome.'"

THE CITY OF HIS DREAMS

Mark Friedberg Designs a Glamorous New York

Mark Friedberg, the production designer for *Wonderstruck*, created the world of 1927 New York. "Research is a big word in the art department. It's the initial influences we find as we're trying to come up with a visual language," he said. "Years ago, I would start by doing research in the library, and it would take me a month to put together a collection of images. But with the Internet I can do the same amount of work in three hours, especially if you know what to look for and how to look. What I'm doing is rewriting the script in images."

Mark Friedberg in front of the facade of the Promenade Theater, which he created on a street in Brooklyn. Even though this will look like 1927 in the movie, behind him you can see glimpses of modern life, like the car and the bicyclist!

A film still of Rose looking at the Promenade Theater.

For Mark, it was important to get the details right, and to show how the two stories—1927 and 1977—compare and contrast. Todd Haynes was working with the idea that 1927 was about New York City building itself upward, and 1977 was about New York City falling down. Mark tried to reflect that in all of his designs. Everything about 1977 is dirty and dangerous, while everything in 1927 is clean, shining, and glamorous.

"Rose sits in her window and stares across the river at New York," Mark said. "She builds a model of it, and tries to imagine what it might be like to be there. To her it's a glamorous, gleaming world that she doesn't live in, but it's what she aspires toward."

The shining city awaiting Rose.

Rose's paper buildings were actually built by many people, including the nine-year-old daughter of one of the producers.

Mark likes to find real locations he can transform into the settings for movies. He grew up in New York City and has designed many movies there. For *Wonderstruck*, he drove director Todd Haynes around the city to scout out locations. Mark said, "I needed to go from exuberant Wall Street in the 1920s to a vacant lot for the 1970s. I also needed to go from the American Museum of Natural History in 1927 to the same museum in 1977. These were transitions that we explored visually."

Filming in the real American Museum of Natural History.

Rose discovers the beauty and wonder of New York City while filming in the Wall Street area.

A model of Times Square was built for the movie. Here you can see a crew member walking on it!

But of course, there are some locations that can't be found in the real world, so Mark and his team built them in a movie studio, from scratch! While much of the movie was filmed on location at the American Museum of Natural History, the meteorite room was re-created in the movie studio. The meteorite looks real, but it's made from wood and plaster!

In the movie, you won't be able to tell what's real and what was created. That's the cinematic magic that a production designer helps create every day.

Workers building a fake meteorite.

The 1927 meteorite room in the movie studio during filming.

TRICKING THE EYE
The Visual Effects of Louis Morin

Louis Morin oversaw the visual effects of *Wonderstruck*, and worked closely with Mark, the production designer. For instance, Mark found a real ferry to film aboard for the scene where Rose travels to New York City. But the ferry in the movie is supposed to be moving *toward* New York, and in fact the ferry Mark hired was docked (and didn't move) in a ferry terminal *in* New York City! So how could the moviemakers create the illusion that the ferry was moving toward a city that wasn't there? That's where Louis Morin and his team of visual effects magicians got to work. Using the latest digital technology, they were able to replace the background with a beautiful view of the 1927 New York skyline that simply wasn't there!

Millie on the ferry before the visual effects.

Millie on the ferry after the visual effects.

A BOOK FOR A MOVIE OF A BOOK

Making the Book *Wonderstruck* for the Movie of the Book *Wonderstruck*

In *Wonderstruck*, a book called *Wonderstruck* plays a big role in the story. I was asked to help create the prop that you see throughout the film. I even invented a fictional author named Dr. Harley S. Perry (Harley is my husband's middle name, and Perry is my middle name!). All the images inside the book are historic illustrations from other books about museums or unusual collections, but one image was made especially for the book. Artist I. Javier Ameijeiras created a beautiful drawing of the Cabinet of Wonders that becomes a focal point of the plot.

This book was created just for the movie.

This is the drawing of the Cabinet of Wonders by I. Javier Ameijeiras.

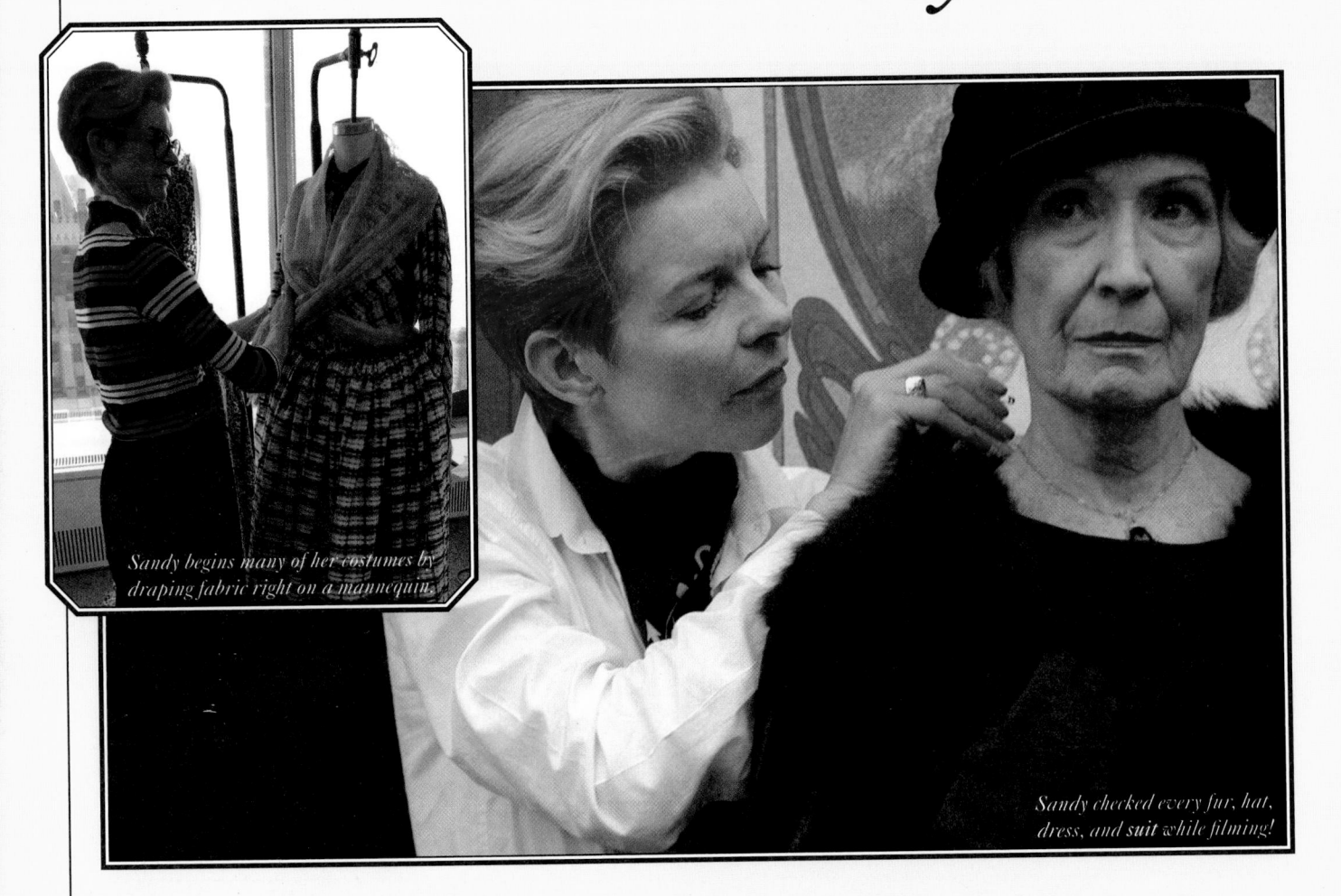

Sandy begins many of her costumes by draping fabric right on a mannequin.

Sandy checked every fur, hat, dress, and suit while filming!

Using Old and New, Sandy Powell
Sculpts the Fashion of the Past

Costume designer Sandy Powell, along with her costume department, created all the costumes for the main characters from scratch. Months before filming started, she researched the time periods and found inspiring visual references in old magazines and silent movies. Then, instead of making drawings (which is what many costume designers do), Sandy "sketched" with fabric. She draped yards of fabric that she liked directly on a dressmaker's dummy. She then cut and sewed the fabric until the clothing began to take shape. Sandy approaches clothing like a sculptor. She understands how different fabrics, colors, and textures work on the body, and on the screen.

EW YORK, 1927
gelo with Fabric

Julianne Moore as Lillian Mayhew, wearing one of Sandy's designs. The costumes had to look good in black and white.

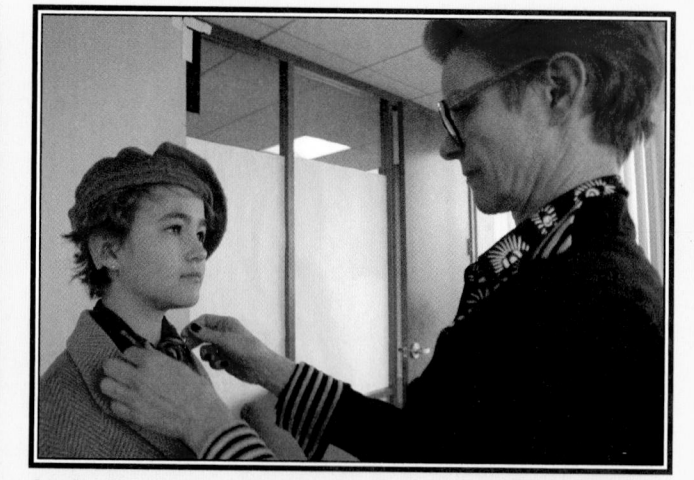

Sandy experiments with different hats and scarves for Millicent Simmonds as Rose.

During filming, Sandy realized this costume for Julianne Moore was too long, so she and her team quickly fixed it!

I have a cameo appearance in Wonderstruck: *I play a writer! Here I am during filming, wearing an original suit from 1927 and real glasses from the time period.*

So many hats!

Clothes from 1927 that Sandy and her team collected for the movie.

To costume all the other actors in the movie, including the hundreds of extras, Sandy handpicked real clothing from the 1920s.

"The world that Rose encounters when she comes to the city is one of wealth and prosperity," Sandy told me, "so as much as possible I wanted everybody in New York in 1927 to be well dressed." When it's time to fit "hundreds of people," she said, "you need hundreds and hundreds *more* items of clothing just to work out who wears what."

Sandy checked every costume for every scene before filming began each day. For each person in the crowd, Sandy asked herself, who can you be? What story can you tell? "Each of these people is part of the story," she said. "Each of these people is a character!"

The crowd of extras.

BY THE LIGHT OF THE SILVERY MOON

Ed Lachman and the Architecture of Light

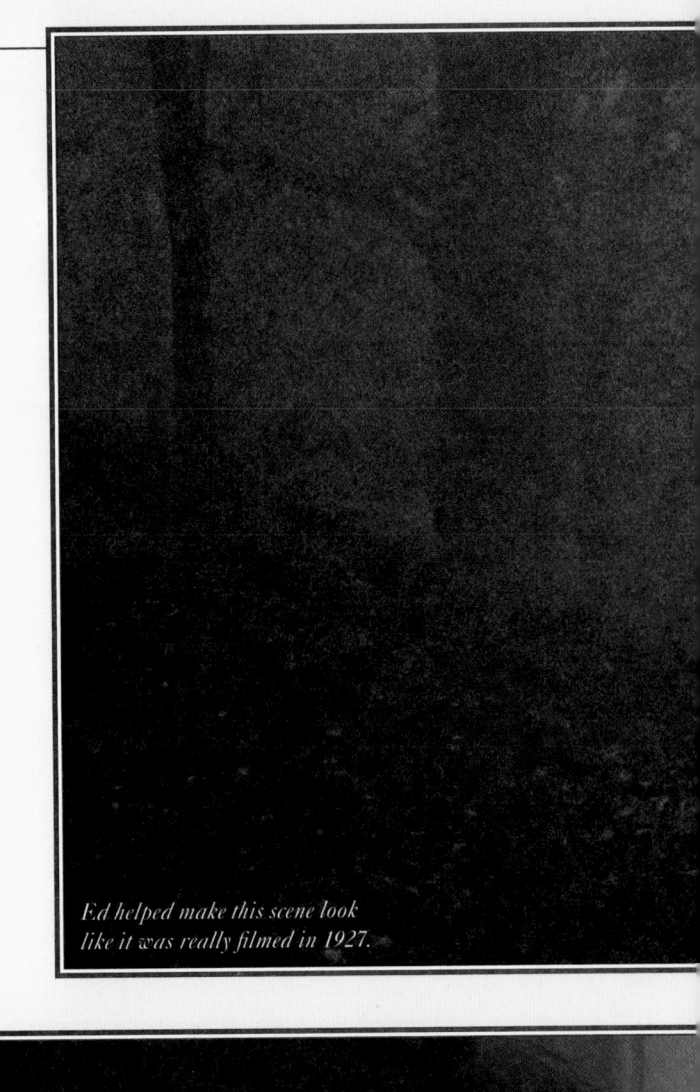

Ed helped make this scene look like it was really filmed in 1927.

Cinematographer Ed Lachman chose the lights, the cameras, the lenses, and then made sure that the footage he shot for 1927 really looked like it was from that time period. He was inspired by old films, and studied them closely so that he could match the style. "In the footage there's a lot of clear compositions and close-ups," Ed explained, so he tried to create that in *Wonderstruck*.

Notice how the light works, where it's coming from, and how it illuminates the scene.

Ed Lachman during the filming of Wonderstruck.

A STAR TRAVE
Julianne Moore Makes

PROMENADE THEATER

PROMENADE THEATER
PRESENTS
LILLIAN MAYHEW
IN

MY
MOTHER'S ADVICE
A DRAMA

Julianne Moore is an Oscar-winning film actress who has worked with director Todd Haynes on four movies. It was Todd's idea to have Julianne play *two* parts in *Wonderstruck*, one character in 1927 and another, very different character in 1977. "I was very lucky!" she said. "And besides being fun for me to perform, it reinforces the idea of family in a visual sense, which we don't always get to see in film."

In the 1927 story, Julianne plays a famous actress named Lillian Mayhew. "To prepare, mostly I watched silent films. Especially the beautiful film *The Wind*, starring Lillian Gish, who we used as the model for Lillian Mayhew." On her first day of filming, Julianne found herself facing a giant wind machine in order to re-create one of her character's old movies, *Daughters of the Storm*. "Oh my goodness, it seems like it would be fun," she remembered, "but in actuality, it is very messy!"

Getting ready to film a scene outside the Promenade Theater. Julianne Moore had to pose for the poster you see on the wall.

LS BACK IN TIME
Her First Silent Movie

Julianne Moore and director Todd Haynes discuss a scene.

Can you find Julianne Moore? She is holding a fake baby. Also note the giant wind machine on the right side!

SIGN OF THE TIMES
American Sign Language on the Set

Back during the silent movie era, Deaf actors were often hired because of their expressive natures; telling a story without spoken language was a natural part of their culture. Hearkening back to this history, six Deaf actors were cast in the 1927 section of the movie, and they all play characters who are *not* deaf! The set of *Wonderstruck* then became bilingual. The Deaf actors used American Sign Language (ASL), while the rest of the cast and crew spoke English. To make it easier for everyone to communicate, several sign language interpreters were always on the set, and Alexandria Wailes, a Deaf actress and teacher, taught a sign language class for the crew before production began.

Interpreter Lynnette Taylor and actress Millicent Simmonds.

Alexandria Wailes leading the sign language class.

Millicent Simmonds waits for a visual cue from her interpreter Lynnette Taylor so she knows when the director has said "Action!"

Alexandria Wailes told me that one of the goals of the ASL class was simply to break the ice. She wanted everyone to know that Deaf people are accustomed to working with hearing people, and they understand that most hearing people are less accustomed to working with Deaf people. "We discussed the different manners in which to communicate if one didn't know how to sign, among them being the use of our phones to type text with each other. I also taught different signs relevant to being on set and topical conversation starters. I think this session was pivotal for everyone who participated."

Because there wasn't enough time for everyone to become *fluent* in ASL, interpreters were important. Lynnette Taylor was the main interpreter on the set, working mostly with Millicent Simmonds, who plays Rose. Lynnette says that the role of an interpreter is about connecting people. "Millie really made connections with everybody on the set."

Actor Howie Seago (left), interpreter Candace Broecker-Penn (front right), and Laura Rosenthal the casting director (wearing white), along with two members of her team chatting in sign language on the set.

Millie and Jaden play a game on set.

On the last day of filming, Millie, Jaden, and Oakes toasted one another with sparkling apple cider!

FRIENDS FROM THE FUTURE

Two Boys from 1977 and a Girl from 1927 Learn to Sing and Sign Adele

Oakes Fegley and Jaden Michael, who star in the 1977 part of the movie, don't have any scenes with Millicent Simmonds, yet the three kids often found themselves together on the set and in the on-set school they attended during filming. They quickly became friends.

"There was a moment I'll never forget," Lynnette Taylor, Millie's sign language interpreter, told me. "I walked into the hair and makeup trailer and saw Millie with Jaden and Oakes. In her lovely Deaf voice, Millie was singing and signing the Adele song 'Hello.' Then Jaden started singing with her; Oakes then joined them!" Lynnette found herself moved by the sight of hearing and Deaf friends all together, communicating and playing. "Wow, this is a moment that shows real possibility," Lynnette remembered thinking.

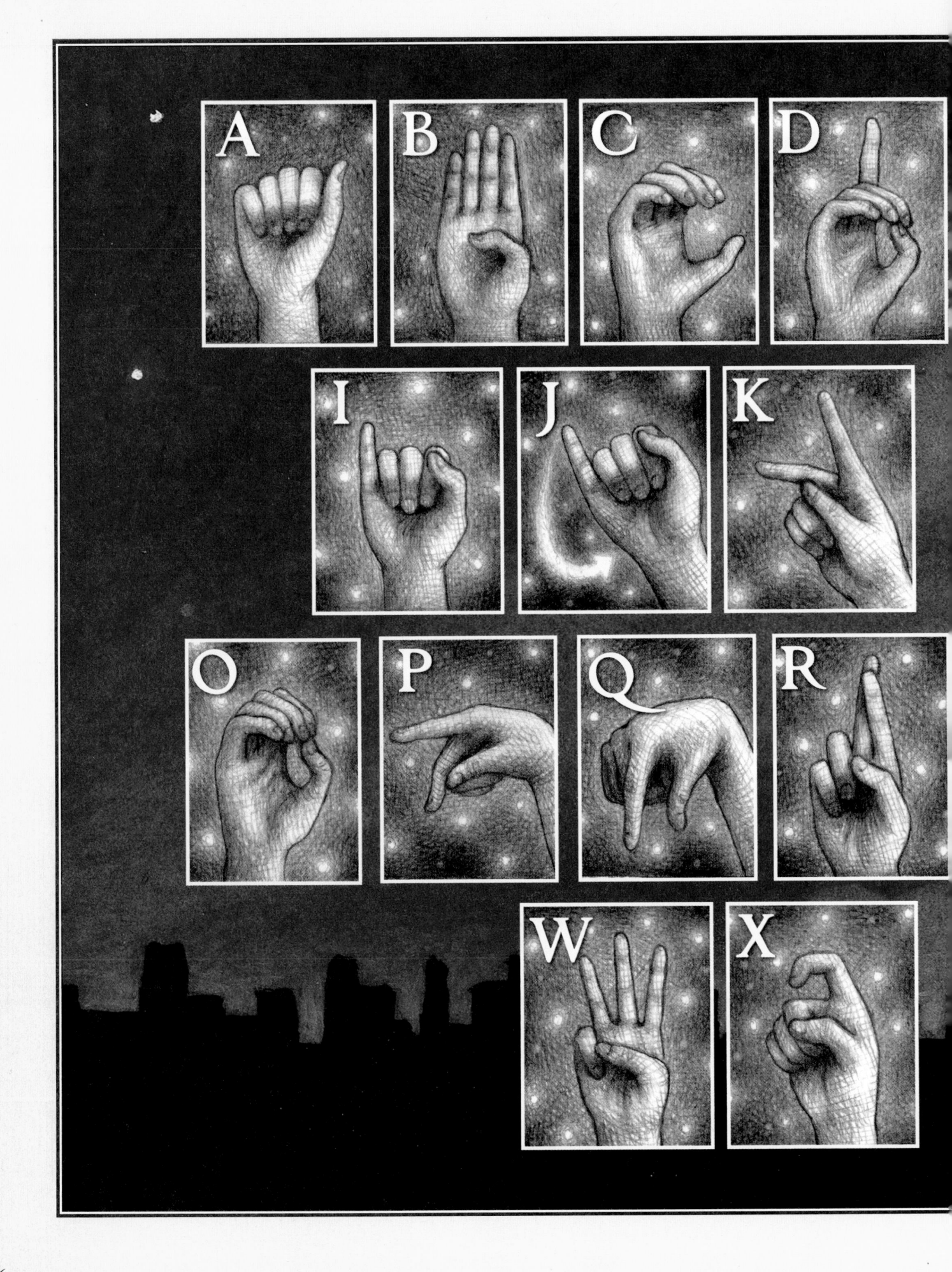

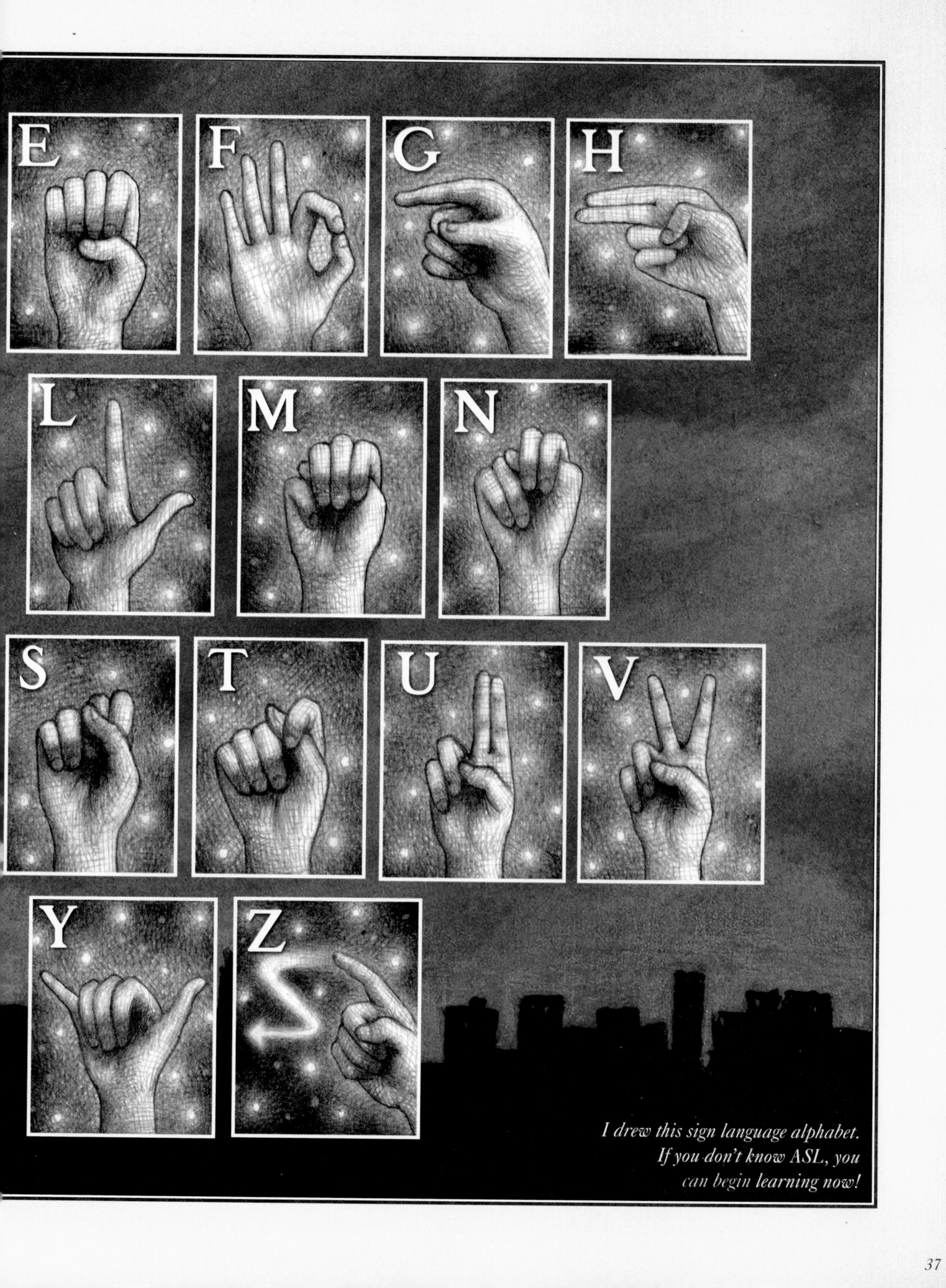

I drew this sign language alphabet.
If you don't know ASL, you
can begin learning now!

37

#DEAFTALENT

Since the entire story of Rose is filmed like a silent movie, we saw an exciting opportunity for Deaf talent. Composer Carter Burwell collaborated with Deaf musician Dame Evelyn Glennie, a famous percussionist whose work can now be heard on the soundtrack. "She made these bits of metal and wood sing," he told me. We reached out to D.J. Kurs the Artistic Director of Deaf West Theater to advise us, and he helped get the word out to the Deaf actors about auditions. In the end, six brilliant actors were hired by casting director Laura Rosenthal. "None of the actors were cast just because they were Deaf," said Laura. "They were cast because they were the best actors for the parts. But because we extended the auditions to the Deaf community, which I've never done before, we discovered this wonderful trove of new talent."

Carole Addabbo as Miss Conrad.

JOHN McGINTY plays the role of Valentin, alongside Julianne Moore's Lillian Mayhew. John recalled the comfort he felt auditioning for the movie. "I had an ASL interpreter in the room, which was a treat and made the audition process so fun and easy." John also loved becoming his character for the screen. "I was fortunate to wear the most beautiful costume ever," John wrote to me. "An eighteenth-century French suitor. It had something like eighteen pieces all together. It took about an hour and half to do hair and makeup!"

CAROLE ADDABBO plays Miss Conrad, an employee at the American Museum of Natural History. "The director and crew signing words such as 'cut' and 'roll' made me feel like I was part of the *Wonderstruck* family. Some crew, prop men, and stage managers could use a little sign language. During our break, Millie, Garrett, and I were chatting with them and taught them a few more signs."

John McGinty as Valentin.

Anthony Natale as Dr. T. M. McGill.

ANTHONY NATALE plays Rose's teacher, Dr. T. M. McGill, the author of a book written to teach Deaf people how to speak and read lips. Anthony told me via an interpreted phone call (Anthony signed on camera to an interpreter, who translated to spoken English for me) that he "jumped up and down for joy" when he was cast as a hearing person, because he always wanted to play a role other than a Deaf character. "I wanted the challenge. I wanted to prove that I can play different roles, so it was an absolute thrill for me."

Anthony was also excited about how this movie might encourage people to work with Deaf actors in new ways. "I think it's going to open up more doors. If there's a role that doesn't require speaking, casting directors could consider a Deaf person to do it. That's something that this movie's going to help show."

LAUREN RIDLOFF plays Pearl, a young woman working as a maid for Rose's father. Lauren tells me, "In the movie, barriers are established loud and clear for the viewers—we know that this is a silent film with no sound. We also know half of the time this film is a talkie with a character who does not hear. But instead of closing anybody off, everybody is invited to cross those barriers to visit, imagine, and be wonderstruck. What a lovely experience it was, working with people who were truthful and fearless about our differences as individuals."

Lauren Ridloff as Pearl.

Howie Seago as the theater director, Remy Rubin.

GARRETT ZUERCHER, who plays Officer Engel, told me about his surprising experience at his first costume fitting. "Upon arriving at the wardrobe department, the crew each spelled their name to me. It made me feel very welcome. I was then led to my dressing room and instructed to try on several different period policeman outfits from 1927. When we finally found a pair that fit me, a tiny woman with bright orange hair was led into the room. I quickly realized that this was Sandy Powell, the costume designer. She looked me up and down and immediately signed to me, 'You need a shirt.' At first, I didn't understand her. Not because her signs weren't clear, but because it was so completely unexpected. I stood there, agog. Here was a three-time Oscar winner signing to me in my native language."

HOWIE SEAGO plays Remy Rubin, the director of a play starring Lillian Mayhew (Julianne Moore). Howie told me that he appreciated working with the other Deaf talent, and "Todd Haynes being as laid-back as he was. He was patient and diplomatic in coaching me to not shout as loud or angry with my first line." Todd also arranged a visual cue with the hearing actors so Howie would know when to say his lines.

Garrett Zuercher as Officer Engel.

"I think the story of *Wonderstruck* will resonate to the outsiders in all of us trying to find our place in this world." — Alexandria Wailes

ALEXANDRIA WAILES, the Deaf actress and teacher, told me that she hopes the movie will have an impact on both hearing and Deaf communities. "Three things about working on *Wonderstruck* have stuck with me. First, the importance of compassion, starting at the top. Second, seeing hearing people on set practice their signing to communicate with Millie, the other Deaf actors, and me. And third, that casting can certainly push the envelope and have Deaf actors take on roles that aren't about deafness."

Alexandria Wailes

Actress Lauren Ridloff and director Todd Haynes with other cast members and sign language interpreter Candace Broecker-Penn (right).

Before filming began, Todd Haynes, Alexandria Wailes, Lynnette Taylor, and assistant director Tim Bird discussed how the Deaf cast, the interpreters, and all the hearing people on the set could best work together.

"If you don't teach your Deaf child to sign, they won't know how to feel. They won't know how to share their feelings with you because it is so hard to communicate. Maybe this movie will help hearing people learn more sign language. Maybe it will also help the Deaf community tell hearing parents with Deaf kids to learn sign language, to know that is what's best for the child."

— Millicent Simmonds

WE ARE ALL CABINETS OF WONDERS

A small model of the Cabinet of Wonders, built by the design team, so they knew what it would look like in three dimensions.

Construction begins.

Painting begins.

One of my favorite parts about writing *Wonderstruck* was doing research into the history of Cabinets of Wonders.

Like the character of Ben, I've always collected things. As a child, I collected glass animals and porcelain figurines, as well as dollhouse furniture and seashells. Now I have even more collections, including glass eyes, miniature Empire State Buildings, snow globes from places I travel, and souvenirs from the 1939 and 1964 World's Fairs. When I was working on *Wonderstruck*, I loved learning that people have been collecting and storing things nearly forever, and that the earliest collectors kept their treasured objects in display cases that came to be called Cabinets of Wonders. Eventually these cabinets grew into entire rooms, and those rooms grew into museums.

When we were making the Cabinet of Wonders for the movie, there was a person in charge of collecting all the items that would be on display in the cabinet. Set decorator Debra Schutt was in touch with collectors around the country, who lent her everything from bird eggs to dinosaur skeletons. Mark Friedberg, the production designer, worked closely with his team to design the most wonderful cabinet, and a group of carpenters and painters spent a month building it from scratch. Then, for a few glorious days, this cabinet stood proudly in a movie studio in upstate New York, where we filmed. This cabinet represents for me all the beautiful work that everyone put into this film, and it illustrates how the movie (and life) is a collaboration between so many people. The finished movie is itself a Cabinet of Wonders, one that Todd Haynes, the rest of the team, and I invite you to explore.

4.

5.

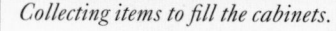

Collecting items to fill the cabinets.

Installing everything.

Todd Haynes shows Millicent Simmonds the finished Cabinet of Wonders for the first time.

Be sure to flip the book over when you're done looking at the finished Cabinet of Wonders on the next page, and you'll leap forward in time to see how the people who re-created the 1920s for *Wonderstruck* also re-created the 1970s. Have fun!

CABINET OF WONDERS

The two stories in *Wonderstruck* are connected by this incredible museum exhibition called a Cabinet of Wonders. Mark Friedberg designed it specifically for the movie. It took months to collect all the items, and this room, as you see it here, existed in the movie studio for only a few days while we filmed.